Managing Remote Teams

A Leader's Guide to Virtual Collaboration

Table of Contents

Chapter 1. Introduction

Welcome to your ultimate leader's guide to mastering the art of remote team management! In this dynamic and eye-opening Special Report, we explore "Managing Remote Teams: A Leader's Guide to Virtual Collaboration". You'll uncover secrets and strategies from the world's most effective virtual leaders, sift through relevant case studies, and gain actionable tips that'll instantly level up your leadership skills in the remote realm. This isn't just another report – it's your ticket to breaking down virtual barriers, supercharging your team's morale and productivity, and evolving into an extraordinary remote leader. If you seek to navigate through the challenges of managing a remote workforce and truly excel in this rapidly evolving digital landscape, then buckle up! This Special Report is crafted just for you.

Chapter 2. Understanding the Dynamics of Remote Teams

Understanding the dynamics of remote teams involves grasping the unique challenges and opportunities that arise when working with people scattered across various geographic locations. From communication breakdowns to differing time zones, remote teams often navigate complicated obstacles. However, with the right understanding and approach, these obstacles can be turned into opportunities for growth, innovation, and increased productivity.

2.1. The Nature of Remote Teams

Remote teams consist of a cohort of employees working together from various geographical locations. These individuals might be in different cities, states, or countries, and they come together to accomplish common business objectives despite the physical distance.

Digital platforms are vital enablers of remote team collaboration. They facilitate communication, project management, and also create a shared workspace in the virtual realm. Such tools might include video conferencing software like 'Zoom', collaborative platforms such as 'Slack' or 'Microsoft Teams', or project tracking apps like 'Trello' or 'Asana'.

A critical aspect of remote teams is that they largely rely on asynchronous communication. Unlike traditional office settings where most communication happens in real time (synchronously), remote teams often have to contend with time zone differences, leading to delays in responses.

2.2. Remote Team Structures

There are several structures a remote team can take, each with its unique dynamics:

Self-Managed Remote Teams: Mostly found in flat organizations where teams are independent and largely guide themselves. These teams have a high degree of autonomy and rely heavily on individual accountability.

Cross-Functional Remote Teams: These teams consist of individuals from different departments or specialties working together to achieve a shared goal. They offer a diverse range of skills and perspectives, making them particularly suited to complex projects.

Global Remote Teams: These teams are disbursed across various countries and time zones. Managing global teams means dealing with cultural differences and communication across wildly varying time zones.

Virtual Project Teams: Formed for a specific project, these teams disband once they achieve the project goals. Virtual project teams often have tight deadlines and a precise purpose.

2.3. The Challenges and Opportunities

With an understanding of the nature and structure of remote teams, it is essential to delve into the unique challenges and opportunities that they present.

The foremost challenge in managing remote teams is communication breakdown. In the absence of physical interaction, crucial non-verbal cues can be lost, leading to misunderstandings. Also, language barriers can escalate when team members hail from diverse geographic locations.

Another challenge is the varying work hours due to differences in time zones. Coordinating team meetings or reaching consensus can be a logistical nightmare. Further, isolation and lack of social interaction can demotivate employees and fuel feelings of disconnection.

However, every challenge presents an opportunity. Remote teams offer flexibility to employees, often leading to a better work-life balance and increased job satisfaction. Thanks to technological advancements, geographical boundaries are shrinking, and companies have access to a global talent pool, making diversity and inclusivity the order of the day.

2.4. Essential Skills for Managing Remote Teams

Effective management of remote teams requires a particular skillset. Leaders must excel at communication, show empathy, bring out the best in every team member, foster a sense of belonging, and instill a culture of trust.

Effective communication is about clarity, consistency, and choosing the right communication channels. Good leaders remember to check-in regularly with their team members, providing clear direction and instant feedback to mitigate any misunderstandings.

Empathy humanizes the remote work experience. A leader with empathy understands the unique struggles each team member may be facing, especially in a remote working setup. They deliver constructive criticism in a careful and kind manner and show understanding when team members encounter challenges that affect their work.

Of all the skills needed to manage remote teams, building trust is arguably the most important. Leaders must trust their teams to deliver in the absence of continual supervision, and teams must trust their leaders to support them.

Fostering a sense of belonging in a remote team might seem challenging, but it's necessary. Regular virtual meet-ups or activities can be organized to encourage team-building. Acknowledging and celebrating individual or team milestones also goes a long way in making team members feel valued and included.

2.5. Tools and Strategies for Remote Team Management

Effective remote team management requires the adoption of tools and strategies that facilitate seamless collaboration, task management, and communication.

Choosing the right digital collaboration platform is crucial. This is a space where team members will spend a significant amount of their working hours. It should be easy to use, inclusive, and comprehensive, supporting video meetings, chats, and document sharing.

In terms of strategies, embracing asynchronicity to overcome time zone hurdles is a wise approach. This means setting expectations about response times and relying on tools that allow for work to happen continuously without real-time intervention from all team members. This way, each team member can work when they are most productive.

Lastly, a culture of transparency should be established. Leaders who are open about decision-making processes and who encourage feedback often build trust among their team members, which is vital for high functioning remote teams.

In grasping the dynamics of remote teams, it's clear that the challenges are vast, but with the right understanding, tools, and leadership skills, these challenges become opportunities for innovation, growth, and enhanced productivity. As the world increasingly adopts remote work, there's no better time for leaders to refine their remote team management practices and thrive in this digital era.

Chapter 3. Crafting a Successful Virtual Work Culture

Establishing a positive work culture has always been crucial for enhancing employee lifestyle, productivity, and retention, but it's even more vital when managing a remote team. A strong, vibrant virtual work culture enriches the employee experience, increases engagement, promotes a sense of belonging and paves the road to high-quality performance – all from the comfort of home.

3.1. Building a Foundation: Shared Values and Vision

The cornerstone of a successful virtual work culture is a shared set of values and a united vision. Leaders must ensure that all team members are aligned with the company's mission. This organizational framework acts as the compass for company policies, work ethics, and behaviour. Understand the values that underpin your organization and articulate them clearly and compellingly to your team. You can reinforce these values through newsletters, company-wide meetings or virtual workshops.

3.2. Regular Communication is Key

Effective communication stands as the life-blood of any remote culture, creating a sense of unity and shared purpose among dispersed team members. Ensure everyone stays updated with relevant information by using a variety of communication tools – emails, video calls, group chats, and project management softwares. Encourage team members to share their thoughts, feedback and queries openly and create an environment that supports and values honesty and transparency.

3.3. Foster Healthy Work-Life Balance

One of the challenges that remote employees often face is maintaining a healthy work-life balance. As a leader, establish guidelines to ensure that personnel don't overwork. Encourage them to draw clear boundaries between their professional and personal lives. Respecting their off-work hours is vital in fostering a healthy virtual work culture.

3.4. Leveraging Technology for Virtual Collaborations

Technology bridges the gap in remote work settings. Spend time researching and investing in the right tools and software to facilitate virtual collaborations. Tools such as Asana for project management, Zoom for video conferencing, and Slack for communication enrich remote interactions, making it easier for your team to connect and collaborate.

3.5. Celebrating Successes and Milestones

- A simple yet effective way of building a positive virtual work culture is celebrating achievements, milestones, or even personal events like birthdays within your team. It helps to foster a feeling of community and also acts as a motivating factor.

3.6. Effective Feedback Mechanisms

Positive feedback can catapult team engagement levels and individual performance. Leverage on regular one-on-one check-ins to understand your team better and provide personalized feedback. You can also use pulse surveys or feedback tools to capture employees' thoughts and sentiments on time.

3.7. Trust and Autonomy

The success of a remote team rests heavily on trust and autonomy. Visa-vis traditional offices, monitoring work of remote employees can be challenging. Establish a trust-based culture where employees are free yet responsible for completing their tasks on time and managing their schedules.

3.8. Virtual Bonding Activities

While remote work offers several benefits, it lacks the social connections found in traditional office settings. Organize regular virtual team-building activities to foster connections. This could be virtual coffee chats, online games, or shared hobby sessions.

3.9. Embracing Diversity

Finally, understand that your team may comprise members from diverse backgrounds. Encourage acknowledging and respecting this diversity. It will not only create a welcoming work environment but also bring varied perspectives and ideas to the table, making your team more innovative and adaptive.

To wrap up, crafting a successful virtual work culture requires intentional effort, time and commitment. It is about building trust, open communication, respect for diversity, and a shared set of values. This way, you can foster an environment that not only encourages productivity but also makes your team feel valued, connected, and motivated.

Chapter 4. Communication Strategies for Remote Leaders

In the modern work landscape, communication is perhaps the most critical skill for remote leaders. Your ability to convey messages clearly, encourage open dialogue, and foster a collaborative online environment hinges on your communication strategies. You are tasked with keeping your remote team connected, engaged, and inspired, and this involves talking and listening in equal measure.

4.1. Understanding the Communication Gap in Remote Teams

In a traditional office setup, communication is often spontaneous and informal. You can pop into someone's office for quick clarification, or grab a coffee and open up a dialogue. Remote settings upend this dynamic, eliminating face-to-face interactions. This can lead to feelings of isolation among team members, and important information can get lost in the transition to virtual communication. It's crucial to understand this communication gap and tackle it head on.

Firstly, recognize that a remote setting impacts not only the quantity but also the quality of communication. Video conferences, for instance, lack the nuances of in-person meetings. They do not provide physical cues, such as body language or tone of voice, which can lead to misunderstandings. It's crucial for a remote leader to consider these challenges and adapt communication strategies accordingly.

4.2. Building a Communication Framework for Remote Work

A clearly defined communication framework outlines when, how, and why communication will occur within the team, creating a sense of structure in the virtual workspace. The first step in creating this framework is to determine which communication channels will be used.

Project management tools like Asana or Trello can keep everyone updated on progress and deadlines.

Ensure everyone in your team understands these channels' roles and uses them accordingly. It's important to provide training if required. Moreover, establish rules regarding response times. For instance, email may require a response within 24 hours, while an instant message might require an immediate reply during working hours.

4.3. Utilizing Asynchronous and Synchronous Communication

Remote communication is either asynchronous (not happening in real-time) or synchronous (happening in real-time). Both modes have their benefits and roles to play.

Synchronous communication, such as video calls, allows for instant feedback and is useful for brainstorming sessions or discussions that need immediate resolution.

As a remote leader, balance these two modes of communication. Encourage deep work and respect personal time by leveraging asynchronous communication but don't let it completely replace real-time, human interactions.

4.4. Active Listening in Virtual Discussions

Active listening is crucial but often overlooked in remote communication. As a leader, this isn't simply about understanding your team members' words, but also about recognizing their emotions and perspectives. You can show you're actively listening by:

Asking follow-up questions to encourage deep dialogue.

Additionally, promote a culture of active listening among your team members. This will help everyone feel heard, fostering greater collaboration and engagement.

4.5. Promoting Openness and Transparency

Transparency builds trust in a remote team. As a remote leader, communicate your expectations clearly and openly, be honest about business challenges, and share regular updates regarding the company's health. Additionally, empower your team by involving them in decision-making processes. This can be done by creating spaces for them to share ideas, and giving them the autonomy and responsibility to implement these ideas.

Being transparent also means acknowledging when you don't have solutions. It's okay not to know everything; what's important is to validate the team's concerns and assure them that you're working on finding answers.

4.6. Encouraging Informal Communication

Informal communication is grounded in the reality that we're all human, and can strengthen the relationship within the team. Create opportunities for informal interaction, like virtual coffee breaks, happy hours, or gaming sessions. These interactions play a vital role in building a thriving remote culture.

While mastering remote communication can be a challenge, it is a cornerstone of successful remote leadership. Adopting these strategies will put you on track to build a highly collaborative and productive remote team. Remember, your team's communication habits reflect your leadership style, so continue to learn, experiment with new approaches, and refine your strategies along the way. You're not only a leader, but you're also a pivotal connector in your remote team's communication network.

Chapter 5. Building Trust in a Remote Environment

Trust is the cornerstone of any successful team, and it is even more critical in a remote setting. With less direct oversight and more independence, a rock-solid trust foundation is essential for a remote team's smooth operation. But how can leaders build this trust?

5.1. The Essence of Trust in a Remote Environment

Trust in a remote setting is not a theoretical construct; it's a practice carried out by team members daily. It underpins the attitude that allows for fluid communication, collaboration, and mutual respect within a team. Key aspects of trust in remote teams include dependability, predictability, and faith in others' competence.

In a virtual setting, where interactions are mostly through screens, trust is heavily reliant on communication. It can be difficult to gauge trustworthiness when physical cues are absent. Consistent and effective communication, therefore, fills this void and builds robust trust landscapes in the virtual world.

5.2. Building Trust from a Distance

Building trust remotely involves a multitude of elements. Here are some key strategies and practices leaders can implement to establish and foster trust within their remote team:

1. **Transparent Communication**: Open and honest communication is a quick route to trust. It's not enough for team leaders to claim transparency; it must be practiced. Regularly sharing updates, company news, and the reasoning behind decisions help breed

openness in the organization. As a leader, promoting receptiveness to questions and fostering an environment that accepts errors as learning opportunities can also contribute significantly.

2. **Clear Expectations**: Each team member must have clarity about their responsibilities, deadlines, and the expected quality of work. This clarity promotes accountability, minimizing misunderstandings and fostering trust. A clear direction also provides a roadmap to success that team members can jointly traverse.

3. **Consistency**: Establishing a rhythm in terms of decision-making, policies, communication, and feedback can boost trust. Inconsistency or sudden changes without proper communication can make team members feel insecure or doubtful.

4. **Regular, Constructive Feedback**. Providing timely, specific, and constructive feedback is crucial for building trust. Not only does it help in recognizing and encouraging positive behavior, but it also guides team members to improve where necessary.

5. **Encouraging Collaboration**: It's beneficial to promote projects or activities that require team collaboration. These collaborations often become the proving grounds for reliability, thereby fostering trust.

5.3. Utilizing Technology to Facilitate Trust

In today's age, there is an ever-increasing number of technological tools that can help facilitate trust within remote teams. However, it's important to remember that technology is a support system and can't replace human interaction.

Here are some strategies for using technology to build trust:

1. **Framework for Regular Communication**: Implementing a virtual communication hub for routine updates and conversations can foster a sense of teamwork. Tools like Slack, Asana, or Microsoft Teams can be used for this purpose.

2. **Virtual Meetings**: Using video conferencing tools can help create a more personal setting and provide visual cues playing a vital role in communication. Regular virtual meetings help in maintaining team cohesiveness and ensuring alignment.

3. **Project Management Tools**: Tools like Trello, Jira, or Basecamp can provide clear visibility of deadlines, responsibilities, and progress, enhancing trust and ensuring accountability.

5.4. Leading By Example

As a leader, you have a unique opportunity to set a strong precedent for trust in your team. By demonstrating vulnerability and openness, you can encourage your team members to do the same.

1. **Show Empathy and Understanding**: Empathy builds a bridge to trust faster than any rule or regulation. Show genuine care for the team members, understand their challenges, and prove that you're there to support them.

2. **Be Accessible and Reliable**: Make yourself available for your team. A reliable and accessible leader cultivates a culture of trust by taking responsibility and being accountable.

3. **Acknowledge and Appreciate**: Recognition and appreciation drive motivation. It indicates that the leader values the efforts and trusts the capabilities of the team member.

5.5. Trust-Building Exercises

Trust-building activities can also be a great tool for strengthening relationships within remote teams. Here are some ideas:

1. **Virtual Team Bonding Activities**: This could include remote team games, virtual meals together, or online movie nights.

2. **Shared Experiences**: Working on a challenging project together, or even participating in an online course as a team, creates shared experiences which can strengthen trust.

3. **Regular Check-ins**: Regular individual and team check-ins can ensure team members feel heard and valued, further contributing to trust.

In conclusion, building trust in a remote environment requires active efforts. Trust can't flourish without a genuine commitment from leaders and teams alike. But with a work culture built on transparency, consistency, empathy, and communication, trust can be the driving force that propels your remote team towards success. Implement the strategies discussed above and keep iterating as per your team's specific needs to foster a high-trust virtual environment. Trust us, the results will be worth the effort!

Chapter 6. Effective Tools and Technologies for Remote Work

The proliferation of digital technologies has made managing remote teams easier than ever before. Yet, the challenge remains to identify which tools will lead to effective and efficient remote work. A myriad of applications exist, each offering unique features and benefits with the potential to facilitate remote work. In this report, we'll delve deeply into the different categories of tools and dissect the top technologies in each category. We'll also provide some insider tips to leverage these tools and technologies effectively.

6.1. Communication Tools

One of the most significant challenges with virtual teams is maintaining clear, robust communication. Lacking face-to-face interaction can lead to miscommunication and misunderstandings. To mitigate these difficulties, leaders must leverage high-quality communication tools.

One top choice is **Slack**, a platform offering instant messaging, file sharing, and group discussion channels. With its clean interface and robust features, such as integrated project management and video conferencing, Slack provides a central hub for team communication.

Zoom is another tool that has gained popularity, particularly for video conferencing. Its robust video features, including screen sharing, a virtual whiteboard, and break-out rooms, provide the means to hold effective virtual meetings.

Microsoft Teams is a comprehensive option, integrating with Office 365, making it ideal for businesses already utilising Microsoft's tools.

Teams offer an efficient way to combine real-time and asynchronous communication in one interface.

Pro tip: Regularly schedule video meetings to foster stronger team relationships.

6.2. Project Management Tools

To coordinate and track the efforts of your remote team, project management tools are invaluable.

Asana offers a visual platform, allowing for easy tracking of tasks in a project timeline or on a virtual Kanban board. It's easy to assign tasks, see what others are working on, and track progress.

Trello utilises a card system, allowing for custom board creations. Each card represents a task, with the ability to add due dates, assign to team members, and classify with tags.

JIRA, specific to the IT industry, is more extensive, serving for issue tracking, project management, and bug tracking.

Pro tip: Accommodate everyone's way of working by using flexible project management tools.

6.3. Document Collaboration Tools

Collaborating on documents in real-time has become a fundamental requirement.

Google Workspace (formerly G Suite) offers collaborative features with Google Docs, Sheets, and Slides. Multiple users can work simultaneously on a document and leave comments.

Office 365 provides similar features with classic Microsoft Office programs like Word and Excel, combined with the benefit of One

Drive cloud storage.

Notion is notable for blending notes, databases, kanban boards, wikis, and calendar views into one unified tool.

Pro tip: Use version control features to avoid confusion with multiple document versions.

6.4. Remote Desktop and IT Support Tools

For tech support or collaborative work requiring a direct interface, remote desktop tools come into play.

TeamViewer allows for remote control, desktop sharing, online meetings, web conferencing, and file transfer between computers.

LogMeIn provides similar options, in addition to digital record keeping and custom branding capabilities.

Pro tip: Find a tool that offers secure and fast remote connections.

6.5. Time Management and Productivity Tools

Ensuring productivity within remote teams requires the right tools as well.

RescueTime monitors computer use and generates detailed reports, offering an eye-opening look at productivity.

Toggl is a dynamic time-tracking tool, offering one-click timers and no-hassle reports.

Pro tip: Use these tools sparingly and trustingly to avoid members feeling micromanaged.

The tools and technologies enlisted here represent a sample of the vast array available to leaders managing remote teams. Leaders should take the time to understand their team's unique needs, and assess tools accordingly. Remember, no tool will be a silver bullet, but with the right combination and a nuanced understanding of their potential, these tools can significantly influence your success in the art of managing remote teams.

Chapter 7. Performance Management in Virtual Teams

Managing the performance of a remote team presents not only unique challenges, but also opens up opportunities for innovative and efficient practices. Perfecting this task requires a comprehensive understanding and application of various techniques tailored to the specific needs and dynamics of virtual teams.

7.1. Setting Clear Expectations

Before any meaningful performance management can be implemented, team leaders must set clear, achievable and measurable goals for their employees. Clear expectations provide team members with the purpose and direction needed to perform effectively on a remote team. These expectations should include defined roles and responsibilities, alongside measurable objectives and key results. In the absence of daily face-to-face interaction, it is essential that these expectations are communicated clearly and frequently, making sure every team member understands their role and the team's goals.

For each task, SMART (Specific, Measurable, Achievable, Relevant, Time-bound) goals are a useful tool. This approach ensures that team members fully understand what's expected of them, the timeframe to complete the task, and how their tasks are correlated with the overall objectives of the team.

7.2. Continuous Communication

Regular and continuous communication is pivotal when managing remote teams. Without it, employees can quickly feel isolated and disconnected. Many virtual team leaders advocate for the use of daily stand ups or check-ins. These daily meetings provide a platform for team members to report their progress towards their goals, any roadblocks they've encountered, and to express their plan for the day.

Leverage tools like Slack, Zoom, and Skype to maintain frequent communication with your team members. Encourage both formal and informal communication to ensure that working relationships, trust, and morale are upheld.

7.3. Periodic Performance Evaluations

Performance evaluations are a must for remote teams. Just as with co-located teams, performance management in virtual teams involves regularly investing time to assess your team's performance. On a monthly, quarterly, or annual basis (depending on your organization's practices), you should sit down with each team member to discuss their performance, progress towards their goals, and areas of improvement.

Digital portfolios or online trackers can be used to monitor performance in real-time. Platforms like Trello, Asana, or Jira help in tracking goals, work progress, and milestones, making it easier to evaluate a remote team member's performance without the need for constant supervision.

7.4. Empowerment and Independence

Empowering your remote team will drastically improve their performance. Encourage ownership of tasks and responsibilities.

This autonomy offers team members a sense of control over their work life and accelerates their decision-making process. It also encourages creativity and innovation, as remote team members often work independently or in smaller groups.

However, it's crucial to strike a balance between autonomy and support. Regular check-ins and availability to provide support or guidance when needed ensures that autonomy doesn't translate into alienation.

7.5. Managing and Aiding Professional Development

Despite not being in the same physical location, managers must ensure team members are continually growing and developing. This may involve providing training or resources, encouraging participation in webinars or professional courses, or even arranging for one-on-one mentoring.

Remember, the growth of individual team members strengthens the overall team and contributes to increased performance.

7.6. Forging a Strong Team Culture

There is no replacement for a strong team culture when it comes to improving the performance of remote teams. It's crucial to replicate an office culture as closely as possible, as it helps keep team members motivated and boosts their engagement levels. Virtual social gatherings, celebrating achievements or milestones, or creating opportunities for team members to get to know each other better can all strengthen the culture of a remote team.

Managing the performance of a remote team is an involved task, requiring specific techniques honed to fit the unique dynamics of virtual teams. It involves setting clear expectations, constant communication, real-time performance tracking, empowerment, supporting professional growth, and fostering a strong team culture. With these tools in hand, a remote team's leader can effectively drive the team towards success.

Chapter 8. Creating and Maintaining High-Performing Remote Teams

Establishing a high-performing remote team starts on an individual level—people need to feel connected to their work, their colleagues, and the company's overarching objectives. This sense of connection is achieved when team members clearly understand their roles and can see how their tasks contribute to the bigger picture.

First and foremost, it's integral to recruit and onboard the right people who are suited to remote work. Understanding that remote work isn't a good fit for everyone is essential. Potential team members should possess certain attributes such as self-discipline, communication skills, and the ability to work independently.

8.1. Recruiting and Onboarding Remote Team Members

When recruiting for remote positions, it's crucial that you look beyond the standard qualifications and professional experience. In addition to specific job-related skills, you should be on the lookout for candidates who display an excellent command of written and verbal communication, show a high level of self-motivation, and the ability to solve problems independently.

The onboarding process presents another opportunity to set new employees up for success. A solid virtual onboarding process includes introducing them to the team, briefing them on key projects, and ensuring they understand the tools and technologies used in their role. It's equally important to outline your expectations clearly, including communication norms, response times, and accountability measures.

8.2. Fostering a Culture of Communication

Communication forms the bedrock of successful remote teams. With a potentially distributed global team across different time zones, ensuring every team member is kept in the loop can be a challenge. Implement daily or weekly virtual meetings to provide updates, acknowledge accomplishments, and address any issues or concerns. Make use of innovative communication tools such as Slack, Microsoft Teams, or Zoom for these live interactions.

Encouraging open and transparent communication also facilitates a stronger sense of community and cuts down on feelings of isolation. A strong culture of communication enables team members to understand how their individual roles contribute to achieving the broader team and company objectives.

8.3. Setting Clear Expectations and Goals

A high-performance team thrives on clarity. This revolves around setting clear expectations regarding tasks, timelines, and communication. All team members should understand what they are expected to deliver and when. Use project management tools like Asana, Trello, or Jira to assign tasks and track progress. These tools also foster accountability, which is vital in remote teams.

Setting team and individual goals helps to maintain motivation and gives a sense of direction. Regularly revisit these goals and adjust as necessary to ensure alignment with business objectives. It should also be clear what the performance metrics are and how team members will be evaluated.

8.4. Offering Support and Resources

Remote employees might not have the same access to resources as those in an office setting. You must ensure that your team has the tools and resources they need to complete their tasks efficiently. This includes remote-access software, collaboration tools, and any necessary training.

Furthermore, it's important to offer emotional and social support. Remote work can lead to feelings of isolation so implementing measures to maintain social contact is fundamental. Regular check-ins, virtual social events, or simply asking how someone is doing can go a long way toward lessening feelings of isolation.

8.5. Celebrating Successes

Recognition and celebrations are a powerful way to boost morale and motivation. Celebrate milestones, acknowledge hard work, and reward achievements, even virtually, whenever possible. This will help to deepen the sense of team spirit, boost morale, and maintain a high level of motivation across the team.

As a remote team leader, your role is crucial in setting up systems and processes that will create and maintain a high-performance remote team. Being proactive in setting clear expectations, fostering open communication, offering necessary resources, and recognizing successes are key aspects in establishing an effective and productive remote team.

Chapter 9. Tackling Challenges in Virtual Collaboration

Navigating through any new terrain calls for a keen sense of exploration, acute observation, and the readiness to tackle unexpected hurdles. Transitioning to a remote model of working involves a similar adventure, encountering new challenges unique to the virtual environment. Let's deep-dive and disentangle these various challenges, and chart a strategic course of action to surmount them.

9.1. The Isolation Factor

One of the main challenges inherent in remote work scenarios is a sense of isolation, which can be emotionally distressing and can adversely affect productivity. Regular check-ins and virtual team events can help overcome this hurdle. Employee assistance programs and mental health services in the form of virtual counseling can also be instrumental in aiding those struggling with isolation.

9.2. Unplugging After Work

Another challenge is navigating the fine line between work and personal time. Without the physical separation between their professional and personal lives, many remote workers struggle to unplug, leading to work from home burnout. Setting robust boundaries between personal and professional time, and upholding a healthy work-life balance are key. Leaders should encourage the team to establish 'end-of-workday' rituals that signal a transition into personal time.

9.3. Persistent Overcommunication

Excess communication can often be a drain on team members, leading to decreased productivity and engagement. Instituting clear rules about what software to use for which type of communication, setting 'no meeting' blocks of time, and designating specific communication-free periods can drastically improve this facet of virtual collaboration.

9.4. Technological Challenges

Yet another challenge unique to remote work is the need to rely heavily on technology. As a leader, you should ensure your team has access to reliable hardware and software. It's equally important to provide training or resources to help team members efficiently navigate this technology. Regular reviews of the tech stack and its effectiveness can keep it in alignment with your team's evolving needs.

9.5. Dissecting Performance Metrics

Performance metrics for remote workers might need recalibration. Traditional methods to monitor on-site employees might not be the best suited for monitoring the performance of remote workers. Rather than monitoring the number of hours worked or availability during the day, the focus should shift to the quality and quantity of work delivered.

9.6. Trust and Accountability

Without day-to-day in-person interactions, building trust and affirming accountability can be challenging. Cultivating a strong culture of trust can be done by assigning clear roles and responsibilities, setting measurable and attainable goals, and providing consistent feedback. Additionally, leading by example can instill a sense of trust and accountability in your team.

9.7. Navigating Time Zone Differences

With remote work, your team could be spread across different time zones, which can make scheduling meetings and collaborating in real-time difficult. Optimal management of time zone differences involves scheduling meetings at mutually convenient times and using asynchronous methods of collaboration when real-time interaction isn't necessary.

Armed with an understanding of these challenges, let's delve into tested solutions and strategies that can help mitigate them, foster a sense of unity, and boost productivity and satisfaction in your virtual team.

9.8. Isolation Countermeasures

Virtual team-building activities, online collaboration tools, and an open communication environment can tackle isolation. Consider having regular video check-ins to facilitate face-to-face interaction, and encourage social conversations in addition to work-related discussions.

9.9. Maintaining Work-life Balance

Establishing a "hard stop" for the workday can help combat the issue of failing to unplug from work. Encourage employees to deliberately disconnect from their work devices and engage in personal activities post-work.

9.10. Overcommunication Solutions

Less is more when it comes to communication in a remote setup. Have a team agreement about how communications will flow – which platforms are best for each type of communication and when to use them. Set guidelines for when immediate responses are expected and when they aren't.

9.11. Technology Hassle-free

Regular IT support, easy access to hardware/software resources, and a frequently updated knowledge base can simplify navigating tech challenges. Emphasize the need for robust internet connectivity and a comfortable home-office setting to boost productivity.

9.12. Performance Metrics Focus

Focusing on work outcomes, like key deliverables or project milestones, instead of hours worked can offer a clearer and fairer picture of an employee's performance. Innovative tools that help monitor remote employee productivity can also be effective in such scenarios.

9.13. Cultivating Trust and Accountability

Foster a virtual work environment where team members feel empowered to take responsibility for their work. Assigning tasks with clarity, providing freedom within guidelines, celebrating achievements, and maintaining transparency can foster trust and peer accountability.

9.14. Optimizing Time Zone Differences

Leverage project management tools that accommodate different time zones, supporting both synchronous and asynchronous collaboration. This could mean having "office hours" for each team member, where they're expected to be online and available.

Addressing these challenges ensures more productive, engaged, and satisfied remote teams. The journey might seem daunting, but the right strategies and understanding of the unique challenges that come with virtual collaboration can make this a rewarding expedition loaded with boundless opportunities for growth and innovation.

Chapter 10. Leadership Skills for a Remote World

In the realm of remote work, where physical proximity is not a luxury, effective leadership morphs from being static and prescriptive to more dynamic and collaborative. One would argue that the rules of engagement have changed. The need for adaptability, communication aptitude, empathy, trust-building, and a people-first approach becomes even more paramount.

10.1. The Evolution of Leadership

In the traditional office context, leadership is often tied to physical presence and power hierarchies. Charles Handy in "Understanding Organisations", highlights command-and-control leaders who gain authority from their position in the organization, stick to procedures, and expect loyalty from their team members.

But in a remote world, a shift in focus is necessary. Command-and-control leadership doesn't thrive. Without physical presence, leaders cannot rely solely on charisma, power hierarchies or micro-management. Instead, leaders must hone specific set of skills, which are critical to steering remote teams towards success.

10.2. Trust

Building trust in remote teams lies at the heart of successful leadership. With physical distance, the need for trust amplifies. We must remember that trust is a two-way street. Leaders must trust their team members to achieve their targets and team members must trust their leaders to provide direction and support.

Tip: As a leader, provide autonomy to your team members but keep them accountable. Use clear expectations and regular check-ins not as a tool for micro-managing, but to provide proper feedback and to re-adjust as necessary. Honest and consistent communication goes a long way in building trust.

10.3. Communication

Effective communication is the lifeline of a remote team too. It promotes collaboration, builds trust, and avoids ambiguity. But, it's not just about pushing information. It's about understanding, encouraging dialogue, and actively listening to your team's needs.

Tip: Over-communicate if necessary. Be clear and consistent in communication. Utilize right digital tools to ensure everyone is on the same page, but remember that technology should assist communication, not complicate it.

10.4. Empathy

Emotional intelligence (EI) becomes even more relevant in a remote setup. Your team members, each in their unique environment, may face different challenges. As a leader, empathy involves understanding these varied challenges and giving personal attention to individual needs while grounding them on shared goals.

Tip: Set aside time for personal check-ins. Understanding your team members' circumstances and acting empathetically can significantly enhance team dynamics and productivity.

10.5. Cultural Competence

Working remotely often brings together global teams. As a leader, navigate through cultural differences and language barriers to establish an inclusive and respectful environment.

Tip: Foster an environment where differences are celebrated and everyone feels valued. Regular team-building activities, celebrations, and recognition contribute towards this cultural competence.

10.6. Adaptability

Lastly, adaptability is critical. The remote world is full of uncertainties. Leaders must be quick to adapt to changes - be it a new technology, a shift in project requirement, or sudden disruption in a team member's availability.

Tip: Stay flexible and resilient. Building a contingency plan and maintaining a growth mindset enables you to steer your team through turbulent times.

In the landscape of remote work, every leader gets to rewrite the rules of leadership that works best for their context. Therefore, experiment, learn from mistakes, adapt, and iterate. This fluidity is what makes remote leadership incredibly challenging yet captivating.

Chapter 11. Future Trends in Remote Team Management

As the world becomes increasingly digital, remote team management is set to undergo seismic shifts. The future of work will be driven by a variety of factors ranging from technological advancements to changing workforce demographics and evolving employee expectations. By understanding and preparing for these trends, leaders can future-proof their remote team management strategies, ensuring their organizations remain competitive and their teams engaged and productive.

11.1. Technological Advancement and Adoption

In recent years, we've witnessed a dramatic increase in the adoption of collaboration tools and platforms. Tools like Slack, Microsoft Teams, and Zoom have become staples, enabling teams to collaborate effectively in real time despite being geographically dispersed.

Artificial Intelligence (AI) is another technology that's set to create a significant impact on remote team management. AI-powered tools will automate repetitive tasks and provide intelligent insights, allowing leaders to focus on nurturing relationships, improving team dynamics and making informed decisions. AI can also improve the hiring process by automating candidate screening and scheduling interviews, reducing time to hire and improving the quality of candidates.

Furthermore, virtual reality (VR) and augmented reality (AR) technologies show significant promise in revolutionizing remote collaborations. These technologies can create more immersive meeting experiences compared to traditional video conferencing, making remote interactions feel more like 'being there.'

11.2. Workforce Demographics and Expectations

Changing workforce demographics will also mold the future of remote team management. Millennials and Generation Z employees, comfortable with digital technologies and looking for flexibility and autonomy, will dominate the workforce. To attract and retain these employees, companies will need to provide flexible work arrangements, including remote and hybrid work models.

Employee wellness will also come to the forefront. As remote work blurs the boundaries between work and personal life, leaders must develop strategies to ensure balance and prevent burnout. This would include training managers to recognize signs of burnout, implementing mandatory time-off policies, and promoting a culture of wellbeing.

11.3. Cultivating a Remote-first Culture

While remote work has many advantages, it also poses challenges to team cohesion and connection. Therefore, cultivating a remote-first culture will be crucial. A remote-first culture is one where all business processes and communication are designed keeping remote employees in mind, ensuring they experience the same level of inclusion and engagement as their in-office counterparts.

Building a remote-first culture involves implementing tools and practices that support effective communication and collaboration, promoting transparency, and fostering a sense of belonging among remote employees. Leaders have a critical role in promoting this culture by demonstrating inclusive behaviors, setting clear expectations, and providing regular feedback.

11.4. The Emergence of Virtual Offices

Virtual offices, where teams can collaborate in a shared digital space, are set to become more prominent. They provide the 'sense of place' that remote work often lacks, strengthening team connection and collaboration.

Virtual offices can be as straightforward as dedicated team channels on collaboration tools or more complex environments enabled by VR/AR technology. Effective use of virtual offices can reduce feelings of isolation in remote teams and foster a stronger sense of team identity.

11.5. Remote Leadership and Team Development

Leadership skills in the remote work environment differ significantly from traditional in-person management. Remote leaders must excel in communication, trust building, and empathy. They need to be adept at managing by objectives, focusing on outcomes rather than monitoring hours worked.

Team development is another significant trend. As teams become more geographically distributed, leaders will need to invest in training and development programs tailored to remote teams' needs. This will involve a blend of e-learning, mentoring, and coaching - all delivered virtually.

11.6. Policies and Legalities of Remote Work

Remote work also brings about new legal and policy considerations. Companies will have to adopt clear policies concerning working hours, overtime, annual leave, and the provision of office equipment for home use. Moreover, they will need to navigate legal complexities, such as tax and labor laws in different countries, in case of internationally distributed teams.

In conclusion, the future of remote team management promises to be dynamic and tech-driven, reflecting larger societal and technological shifts. Through understanding and preparing for these trends, leaders can create a remote work environment that fosters productivity, engagement, and innovation.